Pet Rabbits

Julia Barnes

GARETH**STEVENS**
PUBLISHING
A Member of the WRC Media Family of Companies

Please visit our web site at: www.garethstevens.com
For a free color catalog describing Gareth Stevens Publishing's
list of high-quality books and multimedia programs, call
1-800-542-2595 (USA) or 1-800-387-3178 (Canada).
Gareth Stevens Publishing's fax: (414) 332-3567.

Library of Congress Cataloging-in-Publication Data

Barnes, Julia, 1955-
    Pet rabbits / Julia Barnes — North American ed.
      p. cm. — (Pet pals)
    Includes bibliographical references and index.
    ISBN-10: 0-8368-6781-5 – ISBN-13: 978-0-8368-6781-7 (lib. bdg.)
    1. Rabbits—Juvenile literature.   I. Title.
  SF453.2.B375   2007
  636.932'2—dc22   2006042374

This edition first published in 2007 by
Gareth Stevens Publishing
A Member of the WRC Media Family of Companies
330 West Olive Street, Suite 100
Milwaukee, Wisconsin 53212 USA

This U.S. edition copyright © 2007 by Gareth Stevens, Inc.
Original edition copyright © 2006 by Westline Publishing,
P.O. Box 8, Lydney, Gloucestershire, GL15 6YD, United Kingdom.

Gareth Stevens series editor: Leifa Butrick
Gareth Stevens cover design: Dave Kowalski
Gareth Stevens art direction: Tammy West

Picture Credits:
Oxford Scientific, pp. 4 (Frithjof Skibbe), 5 (Ifa-Bilderteam).
All other images copyright © 2006 by Westline Publishing.

Printed in the United States of America

1 2 3 4 5 6 7 8 9 10 09 08 07 06

Cover: Rabbits are shy animals, and it takes time for them to trust people.

Contents

Words that appear in the glossary are printed in **boldface** type
the first time they occur in the text.

The Wild Side

The European wild rabbit is the ancestor of today's pet rabbits.

The European wild rabbit was one of the most successful of all small animals. Wherever these rabbits lived, their numbers grew quickly because rabbits' needs are simple. Rabbits are **herbivores** that eat grass and plants, and rabbits can make their homes almost anywhere.

The biggest danger rabbits face is from meat-eating hunters. A rabbit is just the right size to be a tasty meal for a medium-sized animal. Rabbits, however, have found safety in numbers. When many rabbits live together, they warn each other of danger, and rabbits are not easy to catch. When a hunter approaches, a rabbit signals an alarm by thumping the ground with its hind leg. The rest of the rabbits then run to the entry of their underground homes.

European wild rabbits lived in Spain and Portugal four thousand years ago.

A fox can run very fast, but it cannot catch a hare that is moving at full speed.

Warren Life

In the wild, rabbits live in family groups in rambling underground homes called **warrens**. A warren has many entrances and exits. It also has sleeping areas and nursery runs for litters of baby rabbits.

When a female rabbit, called a **doe**, is expecting babies, called **kits**, she makes a nest using hair from her underbelly. Her babies are born without fur. Their eyes are closed, and they cannot hear. The kits, however, develop very quickly. Within two months, they no longer need to be cared for, and within five months, the young rabbits are ready to breed.

What Is the Difference?

Hares and rabbits both belong to the **Lagomorpha** family, and they look a lot alike. Hares and rabbits eat the same foods, and they are both hunted by larger meat-eating **predators**. Hares and rabbits, however, have different ways of surviving in the wild.

To escape their enemies, rabbits flee underground. Hares do not dig burrows. Hares rely on speed. Hares have longer legs than rabbits and can run much faster. When a hare is being chased, it can run up to 45 miles (72 kilometers) per hour.

Bunny Bonus

Female rabbits can breed all year round, but they carry their babies in their bodies for only one month. As a result, they can have several litters a year, and the number of rabbits in a warren grows quickly.

The Human Link

People quickly discovered that a rabbit can be a good meal.

People have hunted wild rabbits for a very long time. About the first century A.D., the ancient Romans realized that it was easier to keep rabbits than to go out and hunt them. The Romans built walled enclosures, called **leporaria**, for rabbits, and they bred rabbits for their meat and fur. They valued rabbits so highly that images of rabbits appeared on Roman coins during the reign of Emperor Hadrian in the years 120 to 130 A.D.

Moving On
The **Normans**, who conquered Britain in 1066, also kept rabbits, and they brought rabbits with them to England. The Normans built special rabbit gardens. They put their rabbits in fields where the animals could dig warrens. Then they surrounded the fields with deep ditches and

Rabbits have been used for their meat and fur for two thousand years.

built high banks to keep the rabbits from escaping. The rabbits, however, had no trouble digging their way out, and, in no time, rabbits had spread far and wide in Britain.

When the first European settlers sailed to the New World in the seventeenth century, rabbits went along. Later, other settlers took rabbits to Australia and New Zealand.

Bunny Bonus

Rabbits have been so successful in the wild that they now live on every continent on Earth, except Antarctica.

The Farmer's Enemy

Wild rabbits feasted on farmers' crops, and farmers soon found that these small animals could be big pests. Three rabbits can eat as much grass in a day as one sheep. A large number of rabbits can do terrible damage to a farm. People in many countries have tried to control the number of wild rabbits.

Pet Rabbits

The fashion for keeping rabbits as pets started in England in the nineteenth century. At first, only wealthy people kept rabbits, but today, the rabbit is one of the most popular pets in the world.

Soft and cuddly, rabbits soon became favorite pets.

Perfect Pets

Pet owners of all ages love rabbits. What are the reasons for their great popularity?

- Rabbits are friendly animals and like to be petted by their owners.
- Rabbits are not expensive to buy and do not cost much to keep.
- Rabbits are hardy animals that can live in hutches outdoors.
- Rabbits can also live in cages indoors and can roam free in safe areas some of the time.

- Rabbits are most active in the early morning and in the evening, when their owners are also up, whereas some small animals, such as hamsters, are mostly active at night.
- Rabbits come in many different colors. Owners can choose their favorite colors.
- Rabbits have few health problems and live about eight years.

Rabbits are great pets for people of all ages.

Rabbit Requirements

With their large eyes, big ears, and shy manners, rabbits are extremely appealing. Like all animals, however, rabbits have certain needs. People who want to keep rabbits as pets should be aware of the following:

- Rabbits must be handled gently, and they are easily frightened. For these reasons, rabbits do not make good pets for children under age seven.
- Rabbits need the right foods to stay fit and healthy.
- Rabbits need to exercise outside their hutches or cages.
- Rabbits' hutches or cages need to be kept clean.
- When owners are away for more than a day, they need to find other people to look after their rabbits.

Allergy Alert

Some people have **allergies** to the fur of animals and may suffer with runny noses, watery eyes, or skin problems when rabbits are around. Doctors can test people to see if they have this problem before they get furry pets.

When you own a rabbit, you are responsible for its needs.

A Rabbit's Body

A rabbit's body is more than just a cute bundle of fur.

Nose
A rabbit's constantly twitching nose is a clue to how important its sense of smell is. A rabbit relies on smell to find the best foods, to avoid poisonous plants, and to detect the scents of nearby predators.

Eyes
Rabbits can see behind them and to the sides but not right in front of their noses. Rabbits are also **color-blind**.

Whiskers
A rabbit uses its whiskers to measure the width of tunnels and to find its way in the dark.

Mouth
Rabbits have large tongues and sensitive upper lips, which they use to decide if something is good to eat.

Teeth
A rabbit's twenty-eight teeth grow all the time. They can grow 5 inches (12.5 cm) in a year.

Front Legs
Rabbits use their strong, short front legs for digging.

Ears

Each ear acts on its own and can **swivel** around so a rabbit can tune into sounds coming from any direction. **Lop-eared** rabbits do not hear as well as rabbits with ears that stand up.

Color

The first rabbits had hair with alternating bands of gray and brown, a pattern known as agouti. Pet rabbits now come in dozens of different colors and markings.

Coat

Rabbits may have long, short, or even curly hair. Their coats can feel like velvet or like satin.

Body

Although size and weight depend on the breed, a rabbit's body is generally compact and lightweight.

Tail

Known as the "**scut**," a rabbit's tail is short and upturned, showing pale hair on the underside. Male rabbits, called **bucks**, carry their tails higher than females.

Hind Legs

A rabbit's hind legs are longer than its front legs. The hind legs are very powerful and can kick away dirt when the rabbit is digging. Its longer hind legs give a rabbit a **loping gait**. A rabbit can hop, but it cannot walk or run.

Feet

The soles of a rabbit's feet have pads that provide a firm grip on all kinds of surfaces.

Rabbit Breeds

Today, there are fifty different breeds and many colors of rabbits.

The first pet rabbits looked just like European wild rabbits. They were small, brownish animals with short hair.

Breeders soon realized that they could create more unusual-looking rabbits. Today, rabbits vary in size, have several kinds of ears, and can be any one of a dazzling array of colors.

Most pet owners buy **crossbred** rabbits, which are a mixture of breeds. Some people, however, buy **purebred** rabbits and may even exhibit them in show rings. In the United States, rabbit breeds are grouped according to weight.

The New Zealand White was developed in the United States.

A Dutch rabbit has white markings on its face and the front half of its body.

Heavyweight Breeds

The biggest rabbits were originally bred for their meat and their fur. These large, heavy animals are generally too big for the average pet owner. They include the New Zealand White, which weighs 9 to 12 pounds (4 to 5 kg). Breeders have produced an even bigger rabbit, the Flemish Giant, just for show rings. This breed weighs 25 pounds (11.3 kg).

Middleweight Breeds

Medium-sized rabbits, which weigh about 5 pounds (3 kg), make excellent pets. The most popular middleweight breed is the Dutch. This rabbit makes a good pet for children because it is lively and friendly.

Lightweight Breeds

The Netherland Dwarf is one of the smallest rabbit breeds. These popular rabbits are very active and do not like to be cooped up

A Netherland Dwarf has tiny ears and weighs just 2 pounds (1 kg).

An English Lop's ears may measure 28 inches (70 cm) from the tip of one ear to the tip of the other.

Lop-eared Rabbits

Several varieties of rabbits are lop-eared, which means their ears drop over each side of their heads instead of standing up straight. Many people find these floppy ears especially appealing. The Cashmere Lop's ears are normal-sized, but the English Lop's ears are so long that they trail on the ground.

Coat Types

Short-haired rabbits are the easiest to look after, but pet owners who like grooming may prefer one of the long-haired varieties. Angora rabbits have long, fine, fluffy coats. Angoras shed their coats, and their fur can be spun into silky wool. Rex rabbits have short, dense coats that feel like velvet. A new variety called Astrex is a curly-haired Rex. Satin rabbits were first bred in the United States. Their coats have thin hairs that feel extremely soft and silky. Colors appear darker and richer in Satin rabbits.

A Cashmere Lop's coat is soft, dense, and long.

Colors and Markings

Rabbit breeders have produced some stunning colors and markings. Below are a few of the colors and patterns available.

Smoke Pearl Rex rabbits are a beautiful smoky gray color. Their coats are very short and thick.

- **Blue:** The coats of some rabbits are an even blue-gray.
- **Lilac:** This dove-gray color is very popular.
- **Chocolate:** Some rabbits are an even, warm brown color that looks like chocolate.
- **Sealpoint:** Also known as Siamese, a Sealpoint coat is gray or beige. Sealpoint rabbits have dark faces, ears, legs, feet, and tails.
- **Siamese Smoke:** This color is also known as smoke pearl or blue sable. The rabbits have a blue-gray coat with darker fur on their faces, legs, feet, sides, and tails.
- **Fox:** A rabbit with a white underside is fox-colored.
- **Himalayan:** This all-white rabbit has colored markings around its nose and colored ears, legs, feet, and tail.
- **Dalmatian:** This rabbit has a white body with black spots.

Bunny Bonus

New Zealand Whites are the fastest breeding rabbits in the world. A doe can have five litters a year, with ten kits in each litter.

People make caps, mittens, and sweaters from angora wool.

A Rabbit's Home

Before you buy a rabbit, you need to decide where you are going to keep it.

A pet rabbit can live outdoors in a hutch, or it can live as a house rabbit, free to hop around in safe areas of a home.

The Great Outdoors

Wild rabbits have no problem surviving outdoors, and in most parts of the United States, pet rabbits can live in an outdoor hutch all year round.

This rabbit hutch is the right height above the floor and has a sleeping compartment and spacious living quarters.

- Rabbits need spacious hutches, especially if the rabbit is very large or if two rabbits share a hutch. The smallest size hutch that will work for one rabbit should be 3 feet (90 centimeters) wide, 2 feet (60 cm) deep, and 2 feet (60 cm) high.
- A good hutch has a separate sleeping compartment with a cozy bed of hay. The rest of the hutch should be lined with wood shavings to help absorb the rabbit's urine.
- A water bottle should be attached to the hutch.

- A hutch needs to be 9 inches (23 cm) off the ground to prevent dampness and drafts.
- Living quarters should have a fine wire-mesh front to keep rats or mice from getting in.

Outside Run

A hutch does not give a rabbit very much room to move around. Rabbits need places to stretch their legs and graze. They need to be in an outside run for a few hours a day in all but the very worst weather.

- An outside run should be as big as possible. It should have a shaded area at one end where the rabbit can go if the sun is too hot or if it rains.

- Rabbits need water, so keep a water bottle attached to the inside of the run. Be sure to change the water every day so the water is fresh. Leave a selection of vegetables for the rabbits to gnaw on when they get hungry.
- The run needs to be moved from place to place so the rabbits have fresh grass to eat.

A rabbit needs a chance to move around freely in an outside run. A run also gives a rabbit an opportunity to graze.

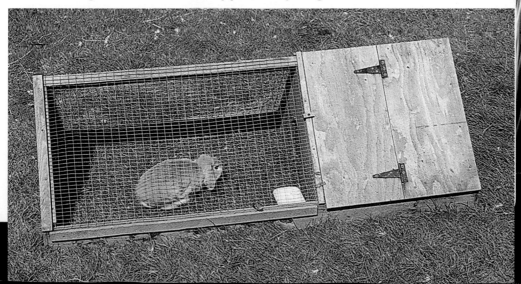

House Rabbits

Keeping rabbits as house pets became popular in the United States in the 1980s.

A house rabbit needs an indoor cage to use as a base.

- A rabbit's cage should be as big as possible. You can buy specially made rabbit cages, or you can adapt a dog crate. The smallest a cage should be for a single rabbit is 21 by 24 by 27 inches (53 by 60 by 68 cm).
- A cage needs a shallow tray on the bottom that can be lined with newspaper or easy-to-clean carpet tiles.

- Most rabbits will use a cat litter box placed in a corner of their cage.
- Washable fleece makes a comfortable bed.
- Attach a water bottle to the inside of the cage.

Bunny-proofing the House

Some people who have house rabbits put them in large playpens to get exercise outside their cages. Most house rabbit owners, however, "bunny proof" a room where their

A house rabbit's cage should have a litter tray, a place for feeding, and a cozy bed.

If you stuff hay into a jar, your rabbit will have to dig it out, which is similar to its natural behavior.

rabbits can hop around safely. Owners need to avoid the following hazards:

- trailing electric cables
- floor-length curtains that are likely to be chewed
- houseplants that might be seen as a tasty snack
- loose wallpaper

Playtime

House rabbits should be given a chance to behave naturally. In the wild, rabbits dig burrows, **forage** for food, and gnaw to keep their teeth in good shape. You can help your rabbit follow its instincts.

- Give it toys to gnaw on so its teeth do not grow too long.

- Hard plastic toys made for teething babies are ideal.
- Make a dig box by filling a cardboard box with wood shavings. Your rabbit can dig among the shavings even though it is indoors.
- To make your rabbit feel as if it is hunting for its food, fill a dog activity ball with small treats. Your rabbit will learn to roll the ball to release the food.

Bunny Bonus

To encourage your rabbit to use a litter box, put about one inch (2.5 cm) of litter in the box, and then add a layer of hay.

The Right Choice

After you prepare a home, you can go out and buy a rabbit!

If you want a purebred rabbit, go to a breeder who specializes in the kind of rabbit you want. If you are happy with a crossbred rabbit, you can find one at your local pet store, or perhaps you know someone whose pet rabbit has had a litter of babies.

Before choosing a rabbit from a pet store, check out the store to make sure the animals are kept in clean conditions. The clerks should be able to help you make a choice. The best time to buy a rabbit is when the rabbit is about six weeks old so it will grow up being used to people.

One or Two?

Wild rabbits live in large family groups, but it can be difficult for pet rabbits living in small spaces to get along.

Two female rabbits often become best friends.

- If you keep a doe and a buck together, you will end up with many babies, unless you **neuter** one of the animals.
- Two bucks kept together will always fight.
- The best plan is to buy two does. Does will live peacefully together and be friends.

Signs of Good Health

Be sure that the rabbit you choose is fit and healthy.

Mouth
Signs of drooling could mean the rabbit's teeth are overgrown.

Eyes
Look for bright, clear eyes.

Ears
Check inside the rabbit's ears to see if they are clean. Dirty ears are usually a sign of ear mites.

Tail
Check under the rabbit's tail for soiled spots or matting, which could indicate diarrhea.

Breathing
Get close to the rabbit to check its breathing, which should be quiet and regular.

Coat
The coat should be clean and glossy, without any scaly flakes or bald patches.

Body
The rabbit's body should have no lumps or swellings.

Movement
Look for the typical bunny hop. Check for any signs of lameness.

If you decide to raise just one rabbit, you must be prepared to keep it company, playing with it and planning different digging and foraging activities. If your rabbit has nothing to do, it will show no interest in its surroundings and may become overweight.

Bunny Bonus

Pet store owners or experienced rabbit keepers can tell you which rabbits are does and which are bucks. Be sure you are getting the kind of rabbit you want.

Making Friends

If you spend time getting to know your rabbit, it will stop being frightened of you and become very tame.

When you first bring your rabbit home, you will want to stroke it and play with it, but you must be patient. For the first couple of days, your rabbit needs peace and quiet to get used to its new home. Your rabbit will start getting used to you because you will be around, providing its food and changing its water. Your rabbit will get to know you without suffering the stress of being handled.

Handling

When your rabbit appears to be happy and relaxed in its new home, you can start making friends.

- To begin with, sit close to the hutch or cage and talk to your rabbit. Do not make any sudden movements.
- Try offering a treat so the rabbit has to come to you and gets used to your hand.

Rabbits are shy animals. It takes takes time for them to trust people.

- Now try stroking your rabbit. Most rabbits love to have their foreheads scratched and will learn to sit perfectly still.
- The next step is to take the rabbit out of the hutch or cage. Ask an adult to help you because rabbits panic easily, and you might drop the rabbit if it starts to squirm.
- As soon as the rabbit is out of the cage, put it on the floor. Rabbits do not like being carried around.
- When your rabbit becomes tamer, try holding it on your lap.

Other Pets

If you have another pet, such as a dog, you will need to be very careful, especially with a house rabbit. To start with, the dog should meet the rabbit when the rabbit is in its hutch or cage. The rabbit will be frightened, so keep the dog at a distance. Reward the dog with a treat if the dog remains calm and well behaved.

Over time, the dog will lose interest in the rabbit, but, to protect your rabbit, you should never allow the dog near the hutch or cage without supervision.

A dog can be trained to live peacefully with house rabbits, but never leave these animals alone together.

Bunny Bonus

If a rabbit needs to be picked up, it should be grasped firmly at the scruff of its neck (just below the ears) with one hand while the other hand supports the rabbit's **hindquarters.**

Rabbit Care

Looking after a rabbit means keeping the rabbit's house clean and watching for health problems.

Cleaning out a cage or a hutch might not sound like fun, but knowing that you are keeping your rabbit as clean and comfortable as possible is very rewarding.

Daily Tasks
- Remove all uneaten food and wash the feeding bowls.
- Refill the water bottle with fresh water.
- Remove wet bedding and droppings. This job is easy if your rabbit uses a litter box.

Weekly Tasks
- Take your rabbit to its exercise area so you can clean its cage or hutch thoroughly.
- Remove all bedding and clean out the cage or hutch with an "animal friendly" disinfectant.
- If your rabbit uses a litter box, remove all litter, clean the box, and refill it with clean litter.
- Remove the water bottle, clean the bottle, and refill it.
- Replace all bedding and surface material.

It is your job to keep your rabbits' home clean and comfortable.

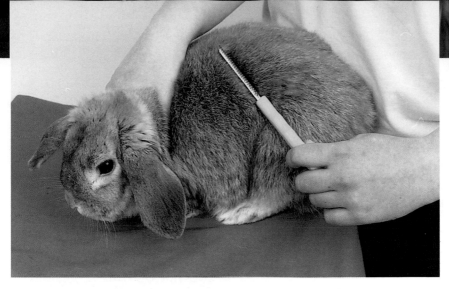

Grooming with a brush and a comb helps remove dead hair when a rabbit coat is shedding.

Grooming

The amount of grooming a rabbit needs depends on the length of its coat. Short-haired rabbits need brushing only once or twice a year when they are shedding. Long-haired rabbits need to be groomed every couple of days to prevent mats and tangles.

Teeth

Keep a close check on your rabbit's teeth to make sure they do not grow too long. If your rabbit drools or has difficulty eating, its teeth may need filing. A veterinarian is the best person to file a rabbit's teeth.

Nails

In the wild, a rabbit keeps its nails trimmed by digging. A pet rabbit's nails may grow too long, and the rabbit may have difficulty hopping around without being uncomfortable. The first time your rabbit needs its nails clipped, you should have a veterinarian or an experienced rabbit keeper do it and show you how.

Bunny Bonus

If you have a long-haired rabbit, start grooming it when it is very young so your rabbit learns to relax and enjoy the attention.

Rabbit Behavior

One of the most rewarding things about owning a pet is learning to understand what the pet is thinking or feeling.

If you have two or more rabbits, you will see how rabbits naturally react to each other. You can also learn a lot about a rabbit by listening to the rabbit's sounds and observing its body postures.

Jumping for Joy

A rabbit expresses happiness by jumping into the air and twisting its head and body in opposite directions. A phrase that describes this movement is "doing the binky."

Lookout Position

When a rabbit stands on its hind legs and seems to be looking out for danger, the rabbit is in a lookout position.

Thumping the Ground

Thumping is an alarm signal to warn other rabbits of danger.

Greeting People

When a rabbit greets its owner by stretching its head forward and flattening its ears, the rabbit is asking its owner to rub its nose.

Playing Dead?

A relaxed, contented rabbit may lie on its side or tummy. In this position, rabbits sometimes look like they are playing dead.

Bunny Bonus

Rabbits often grind their teeth. A rapid, gentle, grinding sound means the rabbit is content. A slow, harsh, grinding sound means the rabbit is in pain.

Rabbits often greet each other with nose-to-nose nudges.

Tiptoeing

When a rabbit moves slowly and with uncertainty, it is worried about its surroundings.

Crouching

A crouching rabbit with its ears flat and eyes bulging is trying to be invisible to a hunter.

Chin Rubbing

Bucks use scent glands under their chins to mark their territory.

Spraying Urine

A buck will spray urine to establish hutch ownership.

Tail Upright

A doe lifts her tail when she is ready for mating.

Tail Out, Ears Flat

A rabbit sticks out its tail and flattens its ears when it is angry.

Spitting

Spitting is a sign of aggression.

Rabbit Sounds

Cooing
A doe may coo to her young, or rabbits may coo to each other when they are relaxed and secure.

Growling
Angry rabbits growl.

Screaming
Frightened rabbits make high-pitched shrieks.

Glossary

allergies: reactions to animal fur or other substances that result in health problems

ancestor: a relative from the distant past

bucks: male rabbits

color-blind: unable to see certain colors

crossbred: of mixed or unknown breeding

doe: a female rabbit

fiber: roughage, such as grass or hay, in an animal's diet

forage: to search for food in the wild

herbivores: animals that eat grass and other plants

hindquarters: back legs

kits: baby rabbits

Lagomorpha: an animal family rabbits belong to

leporaria: Roman walled enclosures for keeping rabbits

lop-eared: having drooping ears that fall on each side of the head

loping gait: moving with long, easy strides

neuter: to operate on an animal so the animal will not be able to breed

Normans: people from Normandy, France, who invaded Britain in the eleventh century

nutrients: substances in food that keep an animal fit and in good health

predators: hunters

purebred: having both parents of the same recognized breed

scut: a rabbit's tail

swivel: to turn in a circle

warrens: underground systems of interconnecting burrows and tunnels where rabbits live

More Books to Read

101 Facts About Rabbits
Julia Barnes
(Gareth Stevens)

All About Your Rabbit
Bradley Viner
(Barron's)

Care for Your Rabbit
RSPCA Pet Guides (series)
(HarperCollins)

**Getting to Know
Your Rabbit**
Gill Page
(Interpet)

Rabbit
ASPCA Pet Care Guides for Kids
(series)
Mark Evans
(Dorling Kindersley)

Web Sites

How to Care for Your Rabbits
www.oink.demon.co.uk/pets/rabbits.htm

The American Rabbit Breeders Association: Breed Photos
www.arba.net/photo.htm

Hopper Home
www.hopperhome.com

Publisher's note to educators and parents: Our editors have carefully reviewed these Web sites to ensure that they are suitable for children. Many Web sites change frequently, however, and we cannot guarantee that a site's future contents will continue to meet our high standards of quality and educational value. Be advised that children should be closely supervised whenever they access the Internet.

Index